My Food O...
Lithuanian C...
Nine of my favourite traditio...

June Molloy Vladička

Text & Photography Copyright © June Molloy Vladička 2013-2017

All Rights Reserved. No part of this publication may be reproduced, distributed or transmitted in any form or by any means, electronic or mechanical, including photocopying, recording, or other by any information storage and retrieval system, without the prior written permission of the author. Exceptions may be made in the case of brief quotations embodied in critical reviews and certain other non-commercial uses permitted by copyright law.

June Molloy Vladička asserts the moral right to be identified as the author of this work.

First Edition, 2017
Second Edition, 2018
ISBN-10: 154323643X
ISBN-13: 978-1543236439

Contact Details:
Website: www.myfoododyssey.com
Mail: june@myfoododyssey.com

Contents

Introduction	2
Kugelis | Potato Pudding	5
Cepelinai |Potato Dumplings	11
Balandėliai | Cabbage Rolls	21
Šaltibarščiai | Cold Beet Soup	29
Koldūnai | Meat Dumplings	34
Rauginti Kopūstai | Sauerkraut	42
Rauginti Agurkai | Half-Sour Pickles	51
Varškės Spurgos | Curd Cheese Doughnuts	58
Kūčiukai | Christmas Eve Biscuits	65

Introduction

This book is, essentially, a love story. A girl walks into a bar, spies a tall and handsome stranger and falls instantly in love. The bar is in a small village in the west of Ireland. The boy is from Lithuania and has only recently arrived in Ireland to work. He doesn't speak much English. She speaks no Lithuanian. Somehow, they make it work. The draw is too strong to resist.

Cooking has always been an important part of communication for me. Despite studying catering and working in the industry for many years I never wanted to be a chef. Cooking is personal. I only do it for people I love. And when regular communication is difficult because of language limitations the language of food becomes even more important.

When we lived in Ireland, Arūnas and I visited Lithuania on a regular basis. I was always delighted to sample traditional Lithuanian dishes and would quiz the cook on how each dish was prepared. This was done through Arūnas, with lots of pointing and gesturing in an attempt to clarify ingredients and processes. Lots got lost in translation. It wasn't really until I moved here and started to eat these dishes more regularly that I really started to get to grips with them. Then, as my Lithuanian improved, I was able to ask more questions, read more books and finally master my own versions of these dishes. It was a labour of love, but it has been worth it.

The dishes in the book are those that I cook on a regular basis.

Because I understand what it is like to attempt these dishes when you have never seen them prepared, or perhaps never even sampled them, I have tried to make them as detailed as possible. I have explained them in the way that I wish they had once been explained to me. Where certain ingredients might not easily be available outside of Lithuania I have suggested substitutions.

These recipes, and the preamble that accompanies them, first appeared on my blog, where they are still available (at time of writing). As they are the most popular recipes on the site I thought people would like the chance to have them together, in one convenient location, and so the idea for this book was born. If you have questions about any of the recipes you can contact me via the blog, e-mail or my Facebook page (see details above). The blog also contains lots of other recipes, stories from my life in Lithuania and lots of photos of the stunning Lithuanian countryside.

June Molloy Vladička

Kugelis | Potato Pudding

Asta walked into the kitchen and sniffed the air, taking in the familiar scent. "Ooh, are you making kugelis?!" she asked excitedly. "I am – I'm testing recipes. How do you make yours?" I replied. Asta wrinkled her forehead in confusion. "What do you mean, how do I make mine? There's only one way to make kugelis." Alas, if only it were so.

Kugelis is a traditional potato pudding that is popular with Lithuanians all over the world. Along with cepelinai, it is one of Lithuania's national dishes and is often served at celebratory occasions such as Christmas and Easter. Also known as bulvių plokštainis, which literally means "potato pie", it is similar to Polish potato babka and a distant cousin of kugel, a Jewish dish which can be made with either chunky potato pieces or pasta.

Like all traditional dishes, recipes for kugelis vary widely both within Lithuania and across the world. The body is made with finely grated (almost puréed) raw potatoes which are usually seasoned and then moistened with steamed milk. Some people include meat, such as diced and fried bacon, chicken pieces, pigs' feet or even pigs' tails. Others prefer to leave out the meat. Some include eggs, which help to set the kugelis, making it easier to slice. Others prefer a softer, more pudding-like consistency and do not add eggs. Of the dozens of recipes I've reviewed and people I've spoken to, I can find little consistency beyond the grated potato.

I've been lucky to have kugelis made for me by a number of friends here in Lithuania. I'm not sure if it's coincidence or perhaps just typical of our region, but all have made it with chicken pieces, usually on the bone, and without eggs. This is the kugelis I fell in love with. While testing recipes I tried several that included egg and can see the merits, principally aesthetically, of adding egg – it makes the pudding much easier to serve. Very little egg is needed to achieve this, so I have settled on using just one egg. I have opted to use boneless chicken as this is easier for serving and eating, but by all means use chicken on the bone if you prefer.

Servings: 4   Prep: 20 mins   Cook: 1 hr   Difficulty: Easy

INGREDIENTS:

100 g | 3.5 oz butter, plus more to grease the dish

1 tsp salt

400 g | 14 oz onion (about 4 medium onions)

1.5 kg | 3.5 lbs potatoes (about 10 medium potatoes)

600 g | 1.5 lb boneless, skinless chicken thighs

¼ tsp garlic powder (optional)

1 egg, whisked

250 ml | 8.5 oz whole milk

METHOD:

1. Preheat an oven to 180°C (355°F)
2. Melt the butter in a medium saucepan over a gentle heat. Add the salt and stir to combine.
3. Peel the onions and chop them finely. Add to the melted butter, stir to coat the onions with the butter, and allow to soften over a very gentle heat for 15 minutes.
4. Meanwhile, peel the potatoes. Grate finely into a large bowl. Add the garlic powder (if using) and whisked egg and stir well to combine.
5. Add the cooked onions, including all of the melted butter, to the potato mixture. Stir well to combine.
6. Heat the milk in a small saucepan over a high heat until it just starts to bubble at the sides. Pour immediately into the potato mixture and stir well to combine.

7. Grease a 2.5 litre (2.5 quart) roasting dish with plenty of butter and arrange the chicken pieces evenly to facilitate easy portioning later.
8. Pour the potato mixture over the chicken pieces and spread evenly. If you like, score the top with the back of a fork to create ridges as the potato cooks.
9. Bake the kugelis for 1 hour. I like the top of my kugelis golden, but if you like yours darker, turn the heat up to 210°C (410°F) for the last 15 minutes of cooking.
10. Allowing the kugelis to cool for 10 minutes before serving makes it much easier to slice as it will set slightly. However, if you just can't wait, feel free to dive in straight away!

Cepelinai | Potato Dumplings

The first time I made cepelinai I failed miserably. And the second time. And probably the third time. After that, I called it quits and resolved only to eat cepelinai that had been prepared for me by someone who knew what they were talking about – either at a restaurant or by one of our Lithuanian friends.

It's not that cepelinai are particularly difficult to prepare, it's just that the concepts were so foreign to me. I was told that they were made with grated potato, so I grated my potatoes the same way I would for hash browns. But that's not what's required. Although many recipes for cepelinai call for grated or even finely grated potato, what they actually mean is pulverized potato. If using a simple box grater you would use the zesting side, not the grating side.

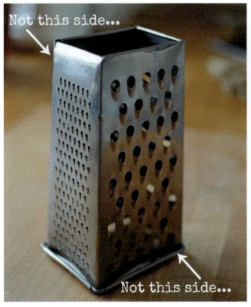

The concept of making a potato dough using a combination of grated raw and cooked potato was also new to me. I thought we Irish ate a lot of potatoes, but our potato-eating habits pale by comparison with Lithuanians. Lithuanians have made potato-eating an art form, with a wide repertoire of dishes based largely around the humble spud.

To the uninitiated, cepelinai (pronounced *sep-elle-in-ay*) are dumplings made with potato dough and a meat, cheese or vegetable filling. They are the national dish of Lithuania, having been prepared here for over 150 years. Originally called "didžkukuliai" (which literally means "big meatballs"), they were rechristened cepelinai early in the 20th century due to their similarity in shape to the zeppelin airships.

Cepelinai are stodgy, hearty fodder designed to feed hungry workers at harvest time or to provide sustenance and warmth during the harsh Lithuanian winters. Calorie-wise, they pack a real punch. A single 200 g dumpling contains 385 g of potato*. This is because two-thirds of the weight of the grated potato is lost when you squeeze out the water. Add to this the fatty mince (ground pork) and the even fattier pork belly, plus a nice dollop of sour cream, and you can see how the calorie-conscious might shy away from them.

Based on my recipe, using a ratio of 60% raw potato to 40% cooked potato.

Despite being the national dish, cepelinai are only prepared in Lithuanian homes on special occasions. They take quite a bit of time and are really only worth making in large batches. They are typically made as a treat for guests or, as mentioned, to feed hungry workers bringing potatoes or hay in from the fields.

Like all traditional dishes, every Lithuanian family has their own cepelinai recipe. If you have a tried and tested recipe that you love, far be it from me to tell you how to make them! This recipe is designed for those who might be new to making cepelinai. As such, I have tried to make it as foolproof as possible and have provided detailed instructions and photos on how to build your dumplings.

After an extensive search both online and in cookbooks I could find no consensus as to the correct proportion of raw to cooked potato for the dough. I know people who make them entirely from cooked potato (adding potato starch to stop them from falling apart) and others who make them almost entirely from raw potato. Having experimented for over a month I have settled on a 60/40 split. (60% or 750 g grated **and strained** raw potato to 40% or 500 g cooked and mashed potato.) This yields a dumpling that is sturdy enough to hold together during cooking but at the same time is soft and not too heavy to eat.

I don't use either egg or onion in the meat mixture. It doesn't need egg to bind it together. In fact, adding egg tends to make the cooked meatballs a little hard. Because the meat is cooked inside the dumpling, even the smallest pieces of onion don't soften and cook in the time. There is plenty of onion flavour in the spirgučiai so there's no need for any in the meat.

Cepelinai can come with a variety of sauces and toppings, but the most common is spirgučiai (pronounced *spir-goo-chay*), made with fried onion and bacon belly (side), and a generous dollop of sour cream. Lithuanian sour cream is very rich, typically being 30-40% fat. You could substitute crème fraîche, lower-fat sour cream or even Greek yoghurt if you prefer.

Servings: 8 dumplings   **Prep:** 2 hrs   **Cook:** 50 mins   **Difficulty:** Medium

INGREDIENTS:

For the potato dough:
- 3 kg | 6 lb 9 oz potatoes
- 2 tsp salt
- Potato starch or cornflour, as required (See method below.)

For the meat filling:
- 500 g | 1 lb 2 oz pork mince (ground pork)
- 1 tsp salt
- ½ tsp garlic powder
- 2 Tbsp cold water

For the topping:
- 250 g | 9 oz smoked bacon belly (side) or pancetta, finely diced
- 400 g | 14 oz onion (about 4-5 medium onions), finely chopped

To cook:
- 2 Tbsp potato starch or cornflour
- 100 ml | ½ cup cold water

To serve:
- 8 Tbsp sour cream / crème fraîche

METHOD:
1. Peel the potatoes, placing the potatoes into a large bowl of cold water as they are peeled to ensure they do not turn brown.
2. Take 500 g | 1 lbs 2 oz of potato, cut into quarters and place in a saucepan. Cover the potatoes with boiling water, place on a high heat and bring back to the boil, then reduce the heat to low, cover with a lid and simmer for 8-12 minutes until the tip of a knife can easily be inserted into the potato pieces. Drain and set aside, uncovered, to cool.
3. While the potatoes are boiling grate or purée the remaining raw potato. If you're not lucky enough to own a specialist potato grating machine, then use either the zesting side of a box grater or purée the potatoes to a very fine pulp in a food processor. If using a food processor you will need to process the potatoes in two batches to ensure there are no small lumps left in the purée.
4. Pour the purée into a large piece of butter muslin or cheesecloth (I use a cotton pillowcase) set over a large bowl. Gather the corners of the material and twist to squeeze out all water from the potatoes. This can take 5-10 minutes depending on the variety of potato and the strength of your hands.
5. When no further water can be squeezed from the grated potato, carefully transfer the dry grated potato to a large bowl. Keep the liquid that came out of the potatoes – you may need this later
6. Using a potato ricer or masher, mash the cooked potatoes until no lumps remain. (Do not add any liquids or fats to the

potato as you might if you were making mashed potato.) Add the mashed potato to the grated raw potato.

7. Add the salt to the potato and mix well with your hands to fully incorporate the ingredients.
8. The resultant dough should be roughly the consistency of play dough – it should form a smooth ball easily but should not stick to your hands. The consistency of the dough is key to the success of your final cepelinai. If it is too wet it will stick to your hands as you form your dumplings. If it is too dry it will crack as you form the dumplings and they may split or fall apart during cooking. If your mix is too dry add a little of the liquid from the grated potatoes, 1 tablespoon at a time, until it reaches the required consistency. If the mixture is too wet, add some potato starch or cornflour, 1 tablespoon at a time, until it reaches the required consistency.
9. In a separate bowl, add the pork mince (ground pork), salt, garlic powder and water. Mix thoroughly using your hands.
10. Divide both the potato dough and meat mixture into 8 equal portions and lay out on a plate or worktop ready for assembly. Form the meat into tight balls the shape of a rugby ball (American football).
11. You are now ready to form your cepelinai. Take a portion of dough and flatten it against the palm of your hand until it is roughly the shape of your hand and just under 1 cm (½ inch) thick, turning regularly as you shape the dough to ensure it does not stick to your hands.
12. Place a piece of meat on the centre of the dough, fold the sides of the dough over the top of the meat and pinch the

dough together firmly to seal the join. Firmly press the dumpling between your two palms, rotating the dumpling little by little, to form the classic zeppelin shape.

13. Ensure there are no cracks on the surface of the dumpling. If you find any cracks, dip your fingertip into the juice from the grated potatoes and gently smooth over the cracks to seal them.
14. Continue with the remaining ingredients until you have assembled all your cepelinai.

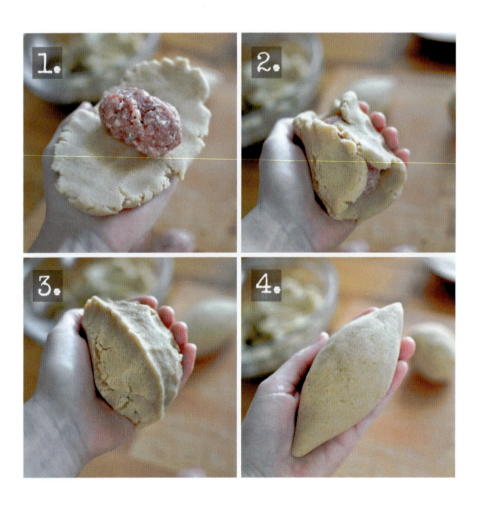

15. Half-fill a 7 litre / 7 quart saucepan, Dutch oven or other large saucepan with cold water and set over a high heat. When the water is boiling, mix 2 tablespoons of potato starch or cornflour with a cup of cold water and add to the saucepan, stirring well as you add the starch liquid to ensure it does not form a gelatinous ball. Adding starch to the cooking water helps to prevent the dumplings from splitting during cooking. It also helps to give the dumplings a smooth, glossy exterior.
16. Carefully add the dumplings to the saucepan. (They will initially sink to the bottom, but will later float to the surface.) Cover the saucepan with a lid, bring the water back to the boil, then reduce the heat to very low so that the water is just barely simmering – if the water is boiling too hard the dumplings might split. Simmer for 45 minutes.
17. While the cepelinai are cooking make the spirgučiai. Add the bacon pieces to a frying pan or saucepan and set over a high heat. There is no need to add any oil or fat as the fat will render from the bacon. When the bacon pieces are golden and starting to crisp, add the onion and reduce the heat to medium. Cook, stirring frequently, until the onions are soft and just starting to turn brown.
18. To serve, carefully lift the cepelinai from the saucepan using a slotted spoon and place on a bowl or plate. Top with a spoon of spirgučiai and a dollop of sour cream.

Balandėliai | Cabbage Rolls

Preparing traditional dishes is never straightforward as everyone has their own view on how they should be prepared. There is nothing more soul-destroying than spending several hours cooking a meal only to get a look from your husband that says "these are not as good as my mother's". I have received that look many times as I developed my recipes for šaltibarščiai, koldūnai and cepelinai. With my balandėliai, I a little fared better – I got "the look" for the first attempt only. After that, something unprecedented happened – I was told they were even *better* than his mother's.

Balandėliai (bal-and-elle-ay) are Lithuanian cabbage rolls stuffed with seasoned pork mince (ground pork) and rice and usually served with a creamy tomato sauce. Balandėliai literally means "little pigeons", so called because of the prevalence of the birds here in spring. The same name (in local language) is used across a number of countries, including Poland, the Czech Republic and Belarus. However, similar dishes can be found in many countries, including the Balkans, Central, Northern, and Eastern Europe, as well as West Asia.

In Lithuania, balandėliai are typically made with white cabbage, which is widely available and inexpensive. I have to admit that I prefer both the taste and texture of balandėliai when they are made with dark green Savoy cabbage. (I also love that the sauce gets caught in the little groves in the leaves!) However, to preserve tradition and to prepare the dish that my husband remembers from his childhood, I am making them here with white cabbage. Feel free to substitute per your own personal preference.

Balandėliai are not particularly difficult to make, but they are a bit fiddly and time-consuming, so I recommend making them in large batches. I generally make about 20 at a time, which is the most that will fit in a single layer into my large Dutch oven.

Most home cooks that I've observed making balandėliai make the sauce by adding ketchup and sour cream to the cooking liquor at the end of cooking, thickening with potato starch as needed. I'm not a fan of ketchup and I also don't like the idea of having to remove all the rolls from the pot to finish the sauce. Instead, I have developed a sauce that replicates some of the tang and sweetness of ketchup, is runny enough to allow the rolls to cook yet thick enough to serve as a sauce without any last minute finishing.

Note that because of the small amount of liquid used in the sauce you need to ensure your saucepan has a tight-fitting lid so the liquid doesn't boil off during cooking.

Servings: About 20 rolls   **Prep:** 50 mins   **Cook:** 1-1½ hr   **Difficulty:** Easy

INGREDIENTS:

For the sauce:

    400 g | 14 oz can of chopped tomatoes

    1 large onion (150 g | 5 oz approx), peeled and cut into chunks

    2 heaped Tbsp sour cream (30% fat*)

    1 tsp salt

    1 tsp sugar

    1 Tbsp apple cider or white wine vinegar

    200 ml | 7 fl oz cold water

*If you use cream with a lower fat content it may split during the long cooking time.

For the rolls:

    100 g | 3.5 oz uncooked white rice such as basmati or long grain*

    1 tsp salt (for cooking the rice)

    1 large head white cabbage (2.5 kg | 5.5 lb approx)**

    700 g | 1.5 lbs pork mince (ground pork)

    ¼ tsp salt (to season meat)

    ¼ tsp garlic powder

    1 tsp onion powder

* If using pre-cooked rice you need 280 g | 10 oz.
** You will not need the full cabbage. However, starting with a large head gives you larger leaves which are easier to roll. Save the remaining cabbage for sauerkraut.

METHOD:

1. Bring a medium saucepan of water to the boil. Add 1 tsp of salt and the uncooked rice. Cover with a lid, return to the boil, then reduce the heat and simmer for 10 minutes (or per package instructions) until the rice is soft. Drain, rinse well with cold water to cool down the rice and place into a colander to drain and cool fully.
2. Cut around the outside of the cabbage about 5 cm (2 inches) from the root. Work your way around a number of times until you have removed the end and part of the heart. Place the cabbage cut-side down in a saucepan and cover with water. Bring the water to the boil, reduce the heat and simmer for 10 minutes. Drain well and set aside to cool. (The cabbage will contain a lot of water, so if you remove it from the pot be sure to put it in a bowl so water doesn't run over your worktop.)
3. To make the sauce, place the onion, tomatoes, salt, sugar, vinegar and sour cream into a food processor. Blitz until smooth. Add the water and blitz again. Transfer the sauce to a large (7 litre / quart) saucepan.
4. In a large bowl, mix the mince (ground pork), rice, garlic powder, onion powder and salt. Mix with your hands until thoroughly combined.
5. When the cabbage is cool enough to handle, gently remove about 20 leaves. Take care not to tear the leaves, but don't worry about small tears or cracks. I find that running a spoon gently under the leaves helps them to come away from the head.

6. You are now ready to roll your balandėliai. Take one leaf and lay it flat on your work surface with the root end towards you. Take about 1 tablespoon of the meat mixture and form it into a roll about 5 cm (2 inches) long. Place the meat just inside the root end of the leaf.
7. Roll the end over the meat until it touches the cabbage behind the meat. Gently fold in one side of the leaf and then the other (as shown in the diagram), then continue to roll to the end of the leaf. Place the roll to one side and continue to roll the rest of the leaves. I find that the outer leaves are a bit easier to roll than the ones deeper in as they have been softened more by the boiling water. Don't worry if some of the leaves crack a little as you're rolling them. Unless they split badly they will stay together during cooking.
8. Arrange the rolls in a **single layer** on top of the sauce. They should be packed tight enough to stop them unrolling during cooking but not so tight that they pop up out of the sauce. Depending on the size of your rolls, you should fit 15-20 rolls into the saucepan. At the start of cooking the sauce should almost cover the sauce, but more liquid will come out of the cabbage during cooking. Resist the temptation to add more water at the early stages or you will end up with a runny, insipid sauce.
9. Place the saucepan on a high heat and bring to the boil, then cover tightly with a lid and simmer gently for 1 hour. Remove one roll from the pot and cut it across the middle. Taste a small piece to see if the cabbage is cooked to your liking. (The

meat will be fully cooked at this point.) The cooking time can vary depending on the type of cabbage used and the size and thickness of your leaves. If they are still a little underdone, replace the lid and cook for a further 30 minutes or until the cabbage is cooked to your liking. If there is less liquid than there was at the start of cooking or if the sauce shows any sign of sticking to the pot, add a small amount of water (about 100 ml | 3.5 fl oz) to the pot before continuing.

10. Serve with boiled potatoes and plenty of the sauce.

Šaltibarščiai | Cold Beet Soup

Growing up I was never a big fan of beetroot. I think this was due to the highly acidic pickled stuff you get in jars, which was pretty much the only type of beetroot available back then. My grandmother used it on all her salads and everything else on the plate would be tinted purple and tainted with its earthy, sour taste.

However, in recent years as fresh, unpickled beetroot has become more readily available, I have become a convert. So when someone gave us a few freshly dug beetroots recently I was absolutely delighted and started thinking about what I'd cook with them.

In Lithuania, there's really only one thing to do with beetroot and that's make cold borscht soup, known in Lithuania as šaltibarščiai (shalt-eh-barsh-chay). This garishly pink soup is incredible popular, particularly in summer when the weather can be quite hot. It is made using a cultured milk called kefir (kefyras in Lithuanian), which is like a cross between yoghurt and buttermilk. Because it is contains high quantities of beneficial bacteria and yeasts, kefir is very good for your digestive system. Couple that with the benefits of eating the "super food" that is beetroot and you have a highly nutritious lunch!

As this is a cold soup it is incredibly quick and easy to make. The only cooking required is for the beetroot. If cooking beetroot seems like too much trouble, or if you can't source fresh, raw beetroot to cook, you can simply use the cooked beetroot that is now available vac-packed in the vegetable section of most supermarkets.

The most difficult aspect of making this soup is probably sourcing the kefir milk. Unfortunately, while widely available in many countries, kefir is not available in all supermarkets. If it's not available at your local supermarket you may find it at Lithuanian, Polish or Russia food stores. Alternatively you can make an approximation using yoghurt and buttermilk, both easily and cheaply available.

Despite being a cold soup, borscht actually makes a fantastic autumn lunch. It has a mild taste but is quite hearty due to the amount of solid ingredients. It would make for a great light lunch on a day when you know you'll be having a heavy or stodgy evening meal. Lithuanian šaltibarščiai is traditional served with a side of warm, boiled potatoes. However, you can replace these with a slice of rye bread or your favourite crusty loaf, as you prefer.

In my original version of this recipe I used my own homemade pickles instead of fresh cucumbers as I liked the zing they brought to the soup. Traditionally, fresh cucumbers would be used. Either will actually work well. In summer I tend to use fresh cucumbers, but off-season I still use pickles if I can't find good quality fresh cucumbers.

Traditionally, šaltibarščiai would not contain lemon juice. However, in an attempt to use less salt in my diet I like to use a small amount of lemon juice to provide a little piquancy. It should not be possible to taste the lemon juice – only to feel a slight bite from its acidity. You can leave the lemon out if you prefer, seasoning only with salt.

Spring onions are not widely available in Lithuania. Lithuanians rarely pull young onions for use in salads. Instead, they cut some of the green stems from onions that are still growing and use only these stems in their salads. The stems regrow quite quickly, so you can cut them again and again until it comes time to lift the onions. We have a few onions in the garden and I used some of their stems in this dish.

Servings: 6   **Prep:** 20 mins   **Cook:** 10 mins   **Difficulty:** Easy

INGREDIENTS:

For the soup:

- 200 g | 7 oz boiled & cooled beetroot (about 2 medium beets)
- 100 g | 3.5 oz cucumber (about 2 large pickling cucumbers, either fresh or pickled – see note above)
- 6 spring onions or 10 green onion leaves
- 2 hard-boiled eggs
- 1.5 litres | 3 pints kefir (or 500 ml | 1 pint thick natural yoghurt and 1 litre | 2 pints buttermilk)
- Bunch fresh dill
- Juice of ½ a lemon (optional)
- Salt to taste

For the side dish:

- 200 g | 7 oz potatoes

METHOD:

1. Peel the potatoes and chop into bite-sized pieces. Place in a saucepan of boiling water, add a good pinch of salt and boil until a knife can easily pierce the flesh.
2. While the potatoes are boiling, assemble the soup.
3. Slice the beetroot & gherkins into fine julienne.
4. Chop the eggs into small dice.
5. Chop the scallions or onions leaves into 1 cm (½ inch) pieces.
6. Finely chop the dill.

7. Pour the kefir into a large bowl or saucepan and add the chopped ingredients and half of the lemon juice, holding back some of the dill for garnish.
8. Taste and season salt and additional lemon juice as required.
9. Ladle the soup into bowls and sprinkle with the remaining dill.
10. Serve the potatoes on a side plate so that they do not heat the soup.

Koldūnai | Meat Dumplings

They say that the way to a man's heart is through his stomach. In my case, this was particularly true. In the early days of our relationship I remember plying my man with rich stews of lamb shanks in red wine sauce served with super-creamy mashed potato, mixed seafood platters served on a lazy Susan with a big bowl of chips and a selection of dipping sauces set in the middle and regular full Irish breakfasts. He still jokes about how he could hear the "chitzzz" of a fresh beer being opened as soon as he set an empty bottle down on the table.

But it worked. Perhaps I'm also interesting, fun-loving, adventurous and whatever else men have on their wish list. But first and foremost I was the provider of damn-tasty meals. Ten years on and still nothing makes me happier than serving my man the food he loves. Since moving to Lithuania I have been attempting more and more traditional Lithuanian dishes. The ingredients are easy to come by and are generally inexpensive and, as I'm exposed to the cooked dishes in friends' houses and in restaurants, I now know what it is that I'm trying to produce.

One of Arūnas's favourite Lithuanian dishes is koldūnai (kol-doon-ay), small dumplings that come with a variety of fillings such as meat, curd cheese or diced mushroom. While these dumplings are quite like Italian ravioli they are not typically served with a sauce. Instead, they come with a generous dollop of sour cream which you then stir through your dumplings, giving them a rich, silky coating and a slight tang. Arūnas loves his served with spirgučiai (pronounced *spear-goo-chay*), made with fried onion and bacon belly (side). The sweetness of the onion and the salty crunch of the bacon pair perfectly with the slippery, subtle taste of the dumplings themselves.

These dumplings are really quite easy to make – rolling the dough is far more straightforward than its Italian cousin, pasta. The dough is softer and can be rolled with a rolling pin or glass – no pasta roller is required. As they're quite small they can be a bit fiddly, so I generally make a large batch and freeze the rest for future meals. The dumplings cook from frozen in minutes, making them ideal for last minute lunches or unexpected guests.

Servings: 75 dumplings   **Prep:** 1-1½ hrs   **Cook:** 7 mins   **Difficulty:** Easy

INGREDIENTS:

For the dough:
- 350 g | 12 oz plain flour (all-purpose flour)
- 2 medium eggs
- 70-100 ml | 2.5-3.5 fl oz water

For the meat filling:
- 700 g | 1.5 lbs pork mince (ground pork)
- 125 g | 4.5 oz fine breadcrumbs
- 3 tsp onion powder
- 1 tsp garlic powder
- 1/2 tsp salt

For the topping:
- 250 g | 9 oz smoked bacon belly (side) or pancetta, finely diced
- 400 g | 14 oz onion (about 4-5 medium onions), finely chopped
- Sour cream

METHOD:

1. Place the flour, eggs and **70 ml (2.5 fl oz) of water** in the bowl of a food processor. Pulse for about 20 seconds to combine. Add more water, a little at a time, as needed to bring the dough together. You want a soft ball that is only very slightly sticky to touch. If you don't have a food processor you can mix the dough in a large bowl mixing with either your hand (as you would pasta) or a metal fork.

2. Wrap the dough in cling film (saran wrap) and rest for at least 15 minutes while you make the meatballs.
3. Place the mince (ground pork), breadcrumbs and seasonings in a bowl. Mix well with your hands to thoroughly combine the seasoning and breadcrumbs into the meat.
4. Using about 1 teaspoon at a time, roll the meat mixture into small balls about 2.5 cm (1 inch) in diameter and set out on a tray or board. Having all the meatballs ready in advance speeds up assembly of the dumplings, helping to prevent the dough from drying out.
5. Cut the dough into two pieces, keeping one half wrapped in the cling film so it does not dry out.
6. Lightly flour a board or table. Using a rolling pin or the side of a glass, roll the dough to a thickness of about 2 mm. (When rolled, each half of the dough should measure roughly 40 cm x 45 cm (16 x 18 inches). If it is not this size then your dough is not thin enough and you will run out of dough.)
7. Using a pastry cutter or glass, cut the dough into rounds about 6 cm (2.5 inches) in diameter.
8. Working quickly so that the dough does not dry out, place a meatball in the centre of each round of dough. Flatten the ball slightly so that it forms a circle with 1 cm (1/3 inch) of dough around the sides. Fold the dumpling in half and pinch the sides of the dough together to seal. The dough is quite stretchy and should be slightly sticky so it should form over the meatball and seal together easily. If your dough doesn't stick together to seal you can dampen one side with water using a pastry brush or your finger. Be very sparing with the

water – you don't want to alter the consistency of the dough.
9. As you make your dumplings line them up on a lightly floured baking sheet or board ensuring that they are not touching. They can stick together quite easily.
10. When you have assembled all the dumplings using one half of the dough, repeat with the other half. (If you roll out all the dough at the same time it will dry out before you can assemble the dumplings.)
11. To prepare the meat and onion topping, place the chopped bacon into a cold pan and set over a medium heat. Slowly render the fat from the bacon, then add the chopped onion and fry for about 8-10 minutes until the meat starts to crisp and the onions soften and start to brown.
12. To cook the dumplings, bring a large saucepan of water to a rolling boil. (As the dumplings are well seasoned I don't add salt to the water. However, you can add some if you like.) Add the dumplings to the pot a few at a time, ensuring they don't stick together.
13. Bring the water back to the boil, reduce the heat and simmer for about 7 minutes. Cut one dumpling open to ensure the meatball is fully cooked before removing the dumplings from the water to serve.
14. Serve the dumplings in bowls topped with the fried bacon and onion and a dollop of sour cream.
15. These dumplings freeze well and cook in minutes from frozen. To freeze, lay the dumplings on a lightly floured baking sheet or other freezer-proof board, ensuring that they are not touching. Place the board flat in the freezer and

freeze for at least 8 hours or overnight, then transfer to a zip-lock bag or freezer box. To cook, follow instructions as above but increase the cooking time to 10 minutes. Again, test for doneness before removing the entire batch from the water.

Notes on ingredients:
1. The quantity of dough given is sufficient for 75 dumplings provided the dough is rolled very thin. The thickness I've used is typical for this kind of dish. However, if you prefer your dough thicker or if you want to ensure you don't run out, you can make a double quantity. Any leftovers can be frozen for next time or cut into strips and cooked like pasta.
2. You can use any kind of meat you like for this recipe – pork, beef, lamb, turkey or even vegetarian meat substitutes.
3. You can also use any kind of breadcrumbs for this recipe. Using different breads will give the meatballs a different taste and texture, so experiment to find what you like. I use Lithuanian medium rye bread which is moist and rich and adds a hint of sweetness to the meat filling.
4. Lithuania is king when it comes to smoked fatty bacon – the array available in supermarkets and farmers' markets is breathtaking. Many people still have a cold smoker in their home and produce fantastic home-smoked meats. You can use any fatty bacon for this recipe, but if you live near a Lithuanian or Polish supermarket I suggest you give their smoked bacon a try.
5. I never use fresh onion or garlic in either meatballs or burgers. No matter how finely you chop them they always

seem to prevent the meat from compacting nicely and the final product takes longer to cook. The meatballs at the centre of these dumplings are particularly small and are cooked quickly, so using the fresh vegetable as an alternative to the powder won't work. If you don't have onion or garlic powder you can either substitute your own favourite dry seasoning (watch out for salt content) or just leave them out completely.

6. These dumplings are quite like Italian ravioli and can be served with grated hard cheese or in any way that you would typically serve meat-filled ravioli.

Rauginti Kopūstai | Sauerkraut

In our house certain things happen so often that they have been given their own name. One of our most frequent occurrences is "where-is-age", a phenomenon whereby Arūnas can't find something he needs, despite the fact that the item is exactly where it's supposed to be. "Where's my wallet?" "It's in the drawer, darling." (Where it always is.) "Where are my keys?" "They're in the drawer, darling." (Where they always are.) You get the gist.

Next on the list is "kickage" (also known as "bounceage"). Arūnas is full of energy and cannot sit or lie still for any length of time, whereas I can sit virtually motionless for long periods, my only movement being the turning of a page or my fingers on the keyboard. His legs appear to have a life of their own, particularly when he's talking. Unfailingly, they move to the beat of his words. Getting through a movie is a nightmare – the legs are crossed, then uncrossed, then crossed again, then tucked under him, then curled to the side. It drives me bonkers.

And then there's "pickleage". Lithuanians love fermented foods, with cucumber pickles, sauerkraut and sour milk or kefir being eaten regularly and in abundance. As luck would have it, I also love fermented foods, so much so that I have a section of my worktop permanently dedicated to fermenting foods. My little fermentation station usually has my sourdough starter, a flask of yogurt and a 3 litre (3 quart) jar of either pickles or sauerkraut. We never, ever run out of fermented vegetables, yet Arūnas still asks at every meal "is there any pickle?"

(I guess I should add that there is also lots of lovage, but we won't talk about that here!)

When the first snow fell recently I rushed out to rescue what was left of my brassicas. I still had lots of cabbage, kale and sprouts growing and wasn't sure how the snow might affect them. My cabbages had started the season as show specimens but had, in later months, been decimated by caterpillars. The remaining heads were unattractively moth-holed. By the time the outer leaves were removed they were quite small and didn't look like they would keep well, so I decided to turn them all into sauerkraut.

Sauerkraut is not a uniquely Lithuanian food, but ingredients do vary from country to country. Traditional Lithuanian sauerkraut contains cabbage, carrot and caraway seeds. Every home cook has their own recipe, but typically there is a much higher proportion of cabbage to carrot. White cabbage is usually used, particularly at this time of year when they are widely and cheaply available.

Sauerkraut is incredibly easy to make – shred or grate your vegetables, add salt and any other seasoning, squeeze the salt into the vegetables to extract the juices and then leave the vegetables, covered in this natural brine, to ferment for several days. There are a few keys to the success of your sauerkraut, though. First and foremost, calculate the quantity of salt carefully. If you want a consistent result you must use a consistent quantity of salt. Estimating the quantity of salt needed will most likely result in a product that is either inedibly salty or limp and bland. I have found

that 2% salt works perfectly, giving us a crunchy, tangy sauerkraut typical of what we might buy in the market. If you're new to sauerkraut-making, I suggest sticking with 2% for the first few batches, and then adjusting up or down to suit your taste.

Your fermentation jar must be spotlessly clean. Fermentation is initiated by organisms naturally occurring on the vegetables, and presence of any competing bacteria may spoil the whole batch. Wash your jar thoroughly with hot, soapy water, rinse well and dry with a fresh cloth. Finally, the fermentation process is anaerobic, meaning it happens in the absence of oxygen. The process does, however, produce gases. Thus, you need to cover your vegetables in such a way that prevents contact with air but allows gases to escape. I find a zip-lock bag perfect for this as it adapts to the size of your jar and the quantity of vegetables. Push the bag down on top of the vegetables, then fill the bag with water to keep the vegetables weighed down under the brine. Any gases produced can escape around the sides of the bag.

Servings: 2 kg | 4½ lb   **Prep:** 15 mins   **Ferment:** 5 days   **Difficulty:** Easy

INGREDIENTS:

- 2 kg | 4.5 lb head white cabbage
- 200 g | 7 oz carrot (1 medium carrot, approx)
- 40 g | 1.5 oz fine salt *(or 2% total prepared vegetable weight)*
- 10 g | 1 Tbsp caraway seeds

METHOD:

1. Peel the carrot. Remove any damaged outer leaves from the cabbage, rinse the whole cabbage under running water and then cut the cabbage into pieces that will fit through the funnel of your food processor, discarding the solid heart. *(You can use a coarse grater for the carrot and a mandolin slicer for the cabbage if you don't have a food processor.)*
2. Weigh the cabbage pieces and the peeled carrot and calculate the exact quantity salt required – 20 g of salt per kilo (1/3 oz per pound) of prepared vegetables. *The sourness of your final sauerkraut depends on the quantity of salt used, so for consistent results do spend a little time calculating this weight correctly.*
3. Shred the cabbage using your food processor's fine slicing disc. Transfer to a large saucepan or food grade bucket. (I use a 7 litre | 7 quart stew pan.)
4. Grate the carrot using your food processor's coarse grating disc and add to the cabbage.
5. Add the salt and caraway seeds.

6. Using your hands, mix the ingredients together and begin to squeeze and massage the vegetables. After just a few minutes you will see liquid starting to come out of the vegetables and notice that the volume of the vegetables is reducing. Continue to squeeze until the vegetables are fully covered with liquid when pressed down firmly. (See photograph.)
7. Transfer the mixture to a clean 3 litre | 3 quart jar. Push the mixture tightly down into the jar until the liquid just covers the top of the vegetables.
8. Fit a 2.5 litre (3 quart) zip-lock food bag into the top of the jar. Put your hand into the bag and push the bag down onto the vegetables and right out to the sides of the jar. Carefully fill the bag with water and zip it closed. The bag will act as a weight to keep the vegetables under the brine and will keep insects and dust out of the jar, but will allow gases that are created during fermentation to escape.

    If you don't have a large enough jar you can leave the vegetables in the saucepan or bucket, weighing the mixture down with a plate and covering with a clean tea cloth.
9. Label the jar with the date so you know when fermentation began. Set the jar on a plate or tray (as some liquid may bubble out during fermentation) and leave at room temperature for a minimum of 5 days.
10. After 5 days test the sourness of your sauerkraut. If it is not quite sour enough, refit the bag and allow to ferment for a further 2-3 days. If you are happy with the sourness you can

transfer the sauerkraut to clean jars or zip-lock bags. Zip-lock bags are ideal as they can be squeezed to remove any air before sealing, regardless of whether or not the bag is full. If using jars, pack the jar as tightly as possible, leaving just a small head space (½ cm | ¼ inch) at the top to minimise air contact.

We go through quite a bit of sauerkraut so I find that 1 litre (1 quart) bags work well for our needs. However, if you only use a little at a time I would recommend storing it in smaller quantities as sauerkraut begins to deteriorate once it is exposed to air.

11. Your sauerkraut will keep for several months if stored in the fridge. It will continue to sour a little as time progresses.

Rauginti Agurkai | Half-Sour Pickles

There are a few condiments that I always have in my refrigerator. The first is mayonnaise – I don't think a day goes by that I don't need it for something, especially in summer. The other is half-sour pickles. Those tangy, crunchy pickles are so versatile, from adorning a burger to adding zing to tartar sauce.

There are three keys to making perfect crunchy, half-sour pickles. Firstly, you need freshly picked, smallish cucumbers. Large cucumbers or those that have been sitting around for days can develop tough skins that are hard for the brine to penetrate and can result in less sour, less crunchy pickles. About 12 cm (4½ inches) long and 3 cm (1 inch) wide is ideal. Secondly, you need to measure your salt to water ratio carefully. Not enough salt and the cucumbers won't ferment, too much salt and the final pickles will be too salty. The quantities of salt I've given are for classic half-sour pickles. Finally, you must allow the pickles time to ferment. Like fine wine, this does not happen overnight. (I've tried lots of recipes for overnight sour pickles and none have worked successfully. If you're in a hurry for your pickles, try overnight marinated pickles instead.) Put the jar somewhere out of your sight for at least 5 days, but ideally leave them for a full week so they reach optimum sourness.

I have split the ingredients list into two groups – basic ingredients and optional extras. Most of the time I just use the basic ingredients because it is quick and easy. This results in a perfect crunchy, half-sour pickle. The optional ingredients are primarily flavour enhancers.

Dill is probably the most common addition, particularly in Lithuania. I'm not a fan of dill so I never use it. Garlic can be overpowering so use it in very small quantities.

The other ingredients are typical of those in shop-bought pickling spices. You can use none, some or all, as you prefer. The cherry leaf supposedly adds to the crunchiness of the pickle. I'm yet to be convinced. Based on my own experience, it is the freshness, size and even variety of the cucumbers themselves that makes the biggest difference to crunchiness.

Note that I never use sugar in my pickles. I know that sugar is common in many Lithuanian half-sour pickle recipes, but I have never found it necessary – my pickles are perfectly crisp and sour without it. I try to limit my intake of added sugars, so if it's not necessary I just don't use it. Note also that the salt content of the brine is 2.5%, which is quite a low concentration in itself. However, the salt content of the pickles is even lower as most of the salt remains in the brine.

Servings: 16 pickles   **Prep:** 10 mins   **Ferment:** 7 days   **Difficulty:** Easy

BASIC INGREDIENTS:

1 kg | 2.2 lbs pickling cucumbers (about 16 cucumbers)

50g | 1¾ oz fine sea salt

2 litres | 2 quarts cold water

Note: I usually make my pickles in larger quantities, especially in summer when I have my own fresh cucumbers from my polytunnel. I use a large (10 litre | 10 quart) bucket and use a dinner plate to keep the cucumbers under the brine. As long as you keep the brine solution at 2.5% (that is 25 g of salt per litre of water) and ensure that the cucumbers are fully covered with the brine, then you can scale this recipe to your needs.

OPTIONAL INGREDIENTS:

1 sour cherry leaf

½ tsp coriander seeds

½ tsp caraway seeds

½ tsp yellow mustard seeds

½ tsp black peppercorns

½ allspice

1 clove of garlic, peeled

1 large sprig of dill

EQUIPMENT:

3 litre| 3 quart jar or food-grade bucket

Zip-lock bag or plate to hold the cucumbers under the brine

3 half-litre | half-quart jars for storing your final pickles

METHOD:
1. Wash the cucumbers, remove any flowers or stems and gently scrape off any prickly spines with the back of a knife. Place the cucumbers into the jar or bucket.
2. Place 25 g (0.9 oz) of the salt in a 1 litre (1 quart) measuring jug. Pour about 200 ml (3 fl oz) of water into the jug and stir until the salt is fully dissolved.
3. Fill the jug up to the 1 litre (1 quart) mark with cold water and stir again. (If you add all the water at the start you have no space in the jug to stir vigorously to dissolve the salt.) Pour the brine over the cucumbers.
4. Repeat with the remaining salt and another litre of water. Pour the brine over the cucumbers until they are fully covered, with an extra 2 cm (1 inch) of brine above the top of the cucumbers. (Note: I have tried making pickles with boiling brine. It does not work as well as using cold brine.)
5. Add some or all of the optional ingredients, if using.
6. Use a zip-lock bag filled with water (see sauerkraut photos for example) or a plate to hold the cucumbers under the brine. The cucumbers must be fully covered throughout the fermentation process or they may begin to rot.
7. Cover the jar lightly with a lid or cloth to keep out insects and dust. Do not tighten the lid – the fermentation process releases gases that must be allowed to escape.
8. Set the jar in a cool place for at least 5 days but ideally for 7 days to allow the sourness to develop. (You can eat the pickles before this if you wish, but they will be salty rather than sour.)

9. When the pickles have reached your desired level of sourness, pour off the brine into a saucepan, then rinse the cucumbers thoroughly to remove any scum. (The scum that develops on the surface of the brine is a completely normal part of the fermentation process and is not harmful. However, it doesn't look very nice or have a nice texture, so it is best to wash it off before eating.)
10. Sterilise 3 half-litre (half-quart) jars using your preferred method. (Options typically include placing the jars in a low oven or putting them through a hot dishwasher cycle.)
11. Arrange your pickles into the sterilised jars. Packing them tightly will help hold them in position under the brine, prolonging their life.
12. Bring the reserved brine to the boil, then carefully pour the brine over the pickles, leaving about 1 cm (½ inch) of headroom at the top of the jar.
13. Put the lids on the jars and tighten gently. The lids will seal as the brine cools.
14. When the jars have cooled check that the lids are fully tightened and label them with the date. The pickles will keep well in the fridge for 4-6 weeks. Once opened, keep in the fridge and consume within 4-5 days.

Varškės Spurgos | Curd Cheese Doughnuts

When I first heard about curd cheese doughnuts I thought they sounded very strange. I had a vision of a chunk of cheddar sandwiched between two sides of a sugary ring doughnut, similar to a filled bagel. I'd been making cheesecake with cream cheese (which is really just curd cheese blended with cream) for years, so I don't know how it was so difficult for me to get my head around. It wasn't until I tasted one of the little fluffy delights freshly made at a farmers' market here in Lithuania that I was sold on the idea.

Lithuanian curd cheese doughnuts are actually much easier to make than their American counterparts as they don't use any yeast and so don't require any time to rise. Instead, they get that wonderful airy centre from a combination of whisked egg and a little baking powder. The batter can be whipped up and ready for frying in less than 15 minutes.

The hardest part about making these doughnuts is probably going to be sourcing Lithuanian style curd cheese. Also known as quark in English, curd cheese comes in a variety of styles and can vary considerably from country to country. Lithuanian curd cheese is quite dry and fine. It is available in many countries in Baltic, Polish, Russian or Eastern European food stores. Look for "varškė" (Lithuanian), "twaróg" (Polish) or "biezpienu" (Latvian). It comes in a variety of packaging, from loose bags to little blocks a bit like Philadelphia cheese.

Recognising that true Lithuanian curd cheese might not be universally available, I set to finding some alternatives. I have often seen Lithuanian curd cheese translated to English as cottage cheese but really the two are nothing similar. Cottage cheese is usually covered in a milky liquid and the pieces are quite large. That said, the tastes are similar so I decided to test the recipe using cottage cheese, strained and mashed to resemble the consistency of Lithuanian curd cheese. The results were not good. While the flavour was similar, the batter was too wet and so the balls did not hold their shape. They were also quite heavy with grease. I tried to adjust the consistency with more flour but the resultant batter was gluey and the doughnuts tough and chewy. My conclusion – cottage cheese does not work as an alternative to Lithuanian curd cheese in these doughnuts.

I asked a group of Lithuanian cooks in the US what they used as alternatives to curd cheese and suggestions included farmer's cheese, ricotta and Spanish queso freso. Unfortunately I couldn't get my hands on any of these to test them, so I can't vouch for the results.

Lithuanian doughnuts are much smaller than American doughnuts and are almost always round balls. They are so light and airy it is very hard to eat just one!

Servings: 20   **Prep:** 15 mins   **Cook:** 7 mins per batch   **Difficulty:** Easy

INGREDIENTS:

For the dough:
- 400 g | 14 oz Lithuanian style curd cheese
- 50 g | 2 oz sugar
- 4 eggs
- 200 g | 7 oz plain flour (all-purpose flour)
- 1 tsp baking powder

To fry:
1 litre | 1 quart sunflower oil

Note that you will need either a deep fat fryer or a sugar (candy) thermometer to perfectly fry your doughnuts.

To serve:
Icing sugar (powdered sugar), for dusting

METHOD:

1. Place the curd cheese, sugar and eggs in a mixing bowl. Whisk together until smooth, pale and creamy – about 5 minutes. *I use an electric hand mixer for this, but you could also use a stand mixer or even a hand whisk. Do not use the blade of a food processor as this will blend the ingredients but not incorporate the air required for a fluffy doughnut.*
2. Add the flour and baking powder and gently fold into the cheese mixture with a metal spoon.

3. Attach a sugar (candy) thermometer to the side of a 2 litre (2 quart) saucepan, add the oil and heat over a high heat until the temperature reaches 170° C (340° F). If using a deep fat fryer ensure your oil is clean and has not previously been used for frying meat or other strong-tasting foods as this will alter the taste of your doughnuts.

4. Taking 1 tablespoon of dough at a time, form the dough into small balls about the size of a golf ball or table tennis ball. This quantity of dough should make 20 40 g (1.5 oz) doughnuts. Use slightly damp hands to smooth the edges of the balls so that they form an even crust.

5. When the oil has reached the required temperature, carefully drop your dough balls into the oil with a metal spoon. Don't overfill the pan as the doughnuts will move about and expand while cooking. For this size saucepan I recommend no more than 4 doughnuts at a time.

6. Cook the doughnuts for 7 minutes, ensuring the temperature of the oil does not fluctuate – adjust the heat as needed to maintain the temperature. Due to the baking powder, the doughnuts will "fizz" quite a bit and move around the pan. They will also turn themselves over several times during cooking, ensuring even cooking on both sides. (If you notice that any of your doughnuts are not flipping by themselves, just tip them over with a metal spoon.)

7. When the doughnuts are cooked, carefully lift out of the oil with a metal spoon. Transfer to a plate lined with a paper towel to drain and cool.

8. Continue to cook the doughnuts in batches until they are all cooked. Note that the mixture keeps well in the fridge for 1-2 days, so if you prefer you can keep some dough and make a fresh batch of doughnuts another day.
9. Allow the doughnuts to cool for at least 20 minutes before eating. This ensures that the outside is dry and crisp and the inside light and fluffy.
10. Just before serving, dust the doughnuts generously with powdered sugar.
11. These doughnuts are best eaten on the day they are made. However, they will keep until the next day if stored in an airtight container once fully cooled. Ideally, don't dust them with sugar before storing, but instead dust them just before serving.
12. When the oil has fully cooled, pour it back into the bottle (or better still, into a glass bottle), close the lid tightly and save for another use.

Kūčiukai | Christmas Eve Biscuits

Christmas is a time for tradition. What's fascinating to me is how much those traditions vary from country to country and even from family to family. Some children post their letter to Santa up the chimney, some through the regular mail. Some leave out milk and cookies for Santa, but in our house it was a bottle of Guinness and a few mince pies. (Clever ole Dad!) Some traditions don't believe in Santa at all.

Being somewhat food obsessed, to me the most interesting differences are centred around the foods we eat and how we prepare and serve those foods. In Ireland, the main Christmas feast is served on Christmas Day and typically includes roast turkey, baked ham, boiled Brussels sprouts and roast potatoes. Sweet treats include iced Christmas cake, brandy-laced Christmas pudding and mince pies. Most of these foods are not traditionally used in Lithuanian Christmas cooking and in many cases are impossible to source here.

In Lithuania, the main celebration is on Christmas Eve. The meal, known as Kūčios, consists of 12 meatless dishes and typically includes herring, sauerkraut, potatoes, mushrooms, beetroot, carrots and stuffed eggs. For dessert there is a stodgy cranberry drink known as kisielius and bite-sized biscuits called kūčiukai (koo-chuck-ay) made with poppy seeds.

Kūčiukai are typically served with a glass of milk. Old traditions dictated that no animal products, including dairy products, should be consumed on Christmas Eve and so poppy seed milk was used in place of dairy milk. In many regions this custom has now petered out and dairy milk is used. In some homes the biscuits are soaked in milk before eating, in others the milk is served as a drink on the side.

Kūčiukai are widely available in the supermarkets here, but they are generally mass-produced and full of unnecessary ingredients. They are incredibly simple to make and only require a small number of ingredients so this year I decided to make my own. I always feel that the tradition of making the food is as important as the food itself. We always made our own Christmas cake and pudding and now that I've chosen to live here in Lithuania I want to start a new tradition of always making my own kūčiukai.

Notes on ingredients:

I use butter in my kūčiukai. Traditionally, only foods typically available during a Lithuanian winter could be used in preparing dishes for the Christmas Eve feast. To me, butter is one of the oldest and most natural cooking fats and fits well with this tradition. Many recipes I found both online and in books used butter as an ingredient. However, if you prefer to stay with the tradition of avoiding dairy products while still using traditional Lithuanian ingredients, I suggest replacing the butter in the recipe with 25 ml (2 Tbsp) of rapeseed (canola) or sunflower oil.

The description of kūčiukai on Wikipedia says that they are made with leavened dough – that is, that the dough has been risen with yeast or some other raising agent. All recipes I found either in books or online included yeast. I made many batches of kūčiukai while developing this recipe and only one batch rose significantly. That batch included more water and the final biscuit was not as crisp as I would like – it was more like a bread than a biscuit. My final recipe still includes yeast as it impacts both the flavour and the texture, but don't expect the dough to double in size as you would with yeast bread. It may rise slightly, or not at all. However, allow it to rest for at least one hour before baking to allow for fermentation of the sugars which will improve both the texture and flavour of your final biscuits.

Poppy seeds are widely available in Lithuania, particularly at Christmas time. They also appear to be widely available in the US. In other countries, they should be available in Health Food stores or in Polish or Lithuanian supermarkets, if you happen to live near one.

Servings: About 100   **Prep:** 20 mins   **Cook:** 18 mins   **Difficulty:** Easy

INGREDIENTS:

250 g | 9 oz plain flour (all-purpose flour)
5 g | 1 tsp salt
90 g | 3 oz sugar
20 g | 2 Tbsp poppy seeds
25 g | 2 Tbsp butter (or 25 ml | 2 Tbsp sunflower oil for vegan version)
7 g | ¼ oz fresh yeast or 3.5 g | ⅛ oz dried yeast
90 ml | 3 fl oz warm water *

*The water should be just warm enough to touch with your finger for at least 10 seconds without feeling hot. I generally use 1/3 boiling water and 2/3 cold water to get just the right temperature.

METHOD:

1. Place the flour, salt, sugar, poppy seeds, butter (or oil) and yeast in the large bowl of your food processor and mix on full power for about 20 seconds to thoroughly combine the ingredients and to distribute the yeast and poppy seeds.
2. Pour the water into the food processor and mix on full power for about 1 minute. The mix should come together into a ball in about 20 seconds but continuing to mix for a little longer will help to knead the dough. After 1 minute the dough should be soft and slightly sticky to touch.
3. Transfer the dough to a lightly floured board and knead for about 1

minute to form into a smooth round. Place the dough in a lightly floured bowl, cover with a clean tea towel and leave in a warm place for at about 1-2 hours to rise and ferment. (Note that the dough will not rise significantly in the same way as yeast bread. However, allowing the dough to rest for 1-2 hours will greatly improve the final flavour & texture of the biscuits.)

4. After 1-2 hours, preheat the oven to 180° C (355° F)
5. Transfer the dough to a lightly floured board and cut into 4 pieces.
6. Roll each piece of dough into a long sausage about 2 cm wide. Ensure the dough is the same thickness along the full length of the roll so that the biscuits will all be a similar size and cook evenly. Note that the roll will end up being about 40 cm long so make sure you have enough space on your board. Alternatively, use your worktop to roll the dough or cut the dough into smaller pieces before rolling.
7. Cut each roll evenly into 2 cm pieces. You should get about 25 pieces per roll.
8. Transfer the pieces to a lightly floured baking sheet. Leave a small gap (about ½ cm) between each piece as they will expand a little during baking.
9. Bake for 15-18 minutes until all the biscuits are golden brown and a little crisp. They will crisp further as they cool so don't overcook them.
10. Cool on the baking sheet before transferring to an airtight jar or biscuit tin.
11. Enjoy with a cold glass of milk or with your favourite coffee.

Printed in Great Britain
by Amazon